A WEEK IN OCTOBER

SAFI SHAMSI

ISBN 979-888521734-7

One day, you'll walk on the road,

as a woman possessed with the confidence of a queen.

With stars glimmering in your eyes,

And fragrance of the lilac green.

You my woman, rise before the sun,
And it's just you until the stars.
Your smile is warmer than sunshine,
And your voice sweeter than the desset wine.

If your skin can't touch mine

In my soul and dreams you'll be

Precious and forever divine,

I've seen your face one thousand times.

That one precious evening, lying restless in bed;

The city all quiet and dead,

I lifted my head up and to my surprise

I found the girl with thousand twinkling stars in her eyes.

Enter Caption

Contents

Preface

They say, "when you meet the love of your life, time stops." When I met her, I knew it was true.

Acknowledgements

Before I thank someone I want to thank this Apple juice, which I'm drinking at the moment. It's really good. It was my dream to write a book for someone who truly deserves it since years and I can't be any grateful for having accompolished the feat. It couldn't have been possible if I had not met her for even once in my lifetime. Yes the girl with the stars in her eyes. The one I wrote this book for. Of course she truely deserved it all as I'd write about her a lote more than I should.

Aditionally my special thanks to one of my juniors from school in helping me set up the book cover as per my requirements. Her artistic skills did come handy.

Prologue

Meeting you wasn't ever easy. I don't really know how we actually came across each other, or was it just the destiny?or was it just that video post? REALLY? I still comprehend how did we even start talking? Especially me. Not that you tried to talk to me many times, not that I was busy either, it's some pure work of destiny and magic that my heart can submit to at the moment, but glad, glad I met you, and I'll be glad for the lifetime. It was all so effortless, that I realised I didn't know what effortless connection felt like.

Every "I love you" you said felt so real and meaningful, made me feel so much loved and the happiest.

At the first meet up I knew I had to meet her again, and yes I did. Why wouldn't I've?

And now I'll be away for three months, certainly not that far, I'll carry all our memories with me, all those sessions when you taught me about people and how I've to change myself from being too much childish to a little less childish, duh.

In what can be called most certain of the times we met, all I could do is thank god, thank every god there is, or ever was or ever will be, and the whole universe.

I barely realised how I went from no phone calls to speaking on the phone daily and now listening to her get drunk and laugh while me staring at the calendar, counting the days when I'd get to meet her again.

CHAPTER ONE

THE LOVE CALLING

8/10/2021

One day from now I'll be with her, yes the girl I love the most, the girl I see my future with, the girl whenever I look at makes me feel the happiest, the girl who's like a cool breeze on a summer noon taking away all the momentary thoughts. Certainly someone who'd make me feel I surround the world than the world surrounds me.

We've been together for around seven months and everything is just perfect. I genuinely see her being in my life for a long time, completing each other. She has really been impactful, made me change my perspectives to certain things which I wouldn't have without her, and everything she does, fills me with immense pride.

I'm excited, this excited that I've already started sorting my outfits for each day I'm supposed to meet her. Yes I should look good, right?

She texts me, "one-day Safi, just twenty-four hours and you'll be here with me, I want to hug you tight. I love you".

I woke up to this message, all happy, happier than any day, yes. I've been told entire life that I need to love myself before I can love someone, I need to heal before I can love someone but the day I started loving her, the notion hasn't been the same anymore. Evidently, the notion was never true, it's pretty bookish, and I don't regret loving at all. I love her and saying "love yourself before you love others" is stupid because once can learn to love themselves by loving someone else. These old poets ain't shit I'd rather say.

CHAPTER TWO

THE SUNSET

9/10/2021

Today is certainly my first ever solo trip and I for obvious reasons am so much excited. Travelling is fun, where one doesn't expect anything from anywhere or anyone.And then, whatever happens is a surprise. The most insignificant thing can become a subject of interest thereby submitting to good memories.

There's this old man in the train who has a seat right beside me, he sounds pretty much fun with a beguiling air of innocence, endearing indeed. He seems to be pretty much enjoying his privileges. I am writing a book review for my previous read,"The kite runner" which he saw me working on, and came up with this obvious question. "Do you write,kid?"

"Yes! I replied with that feeling of not being alone anymore. Yes, you are not alone when you find people with same interests as yours. I introduced myself and made him read my poems that were already published in few national magazines of seafarers.

I have reached the place I've longed for nights. I feel like a newly freed bird from a cage, so much to explore and so much beautiful to come.

I was listening to this song during my journey and it reminded me of the dance video of her she once had showed me and caught myself going in the past — at every beat I was thinking of how gracefully she moved, the way she smiled, the way she raised her eyebrows, how seamlessly her steps matched the lyrics and how beautiful she looked, the most beautiful in the world indeed.

"You know I didn't only like it, but it stuck with me for so long that I couldn't listen to the song without remembering you."

There is no Love at one moment, but when you spend enough time with someone, and like doing it so much that you wish for more, perhaps the feelings get stronger. And I don't know at what point you start calling it Love.

I went to meet her in whatever I was wearing. After all I was meeting her for the first time. Excitement was natural. And their she was siting in front of me. Like a diva. I could not trust my eyes that she is that alluring. Time stopped, I felt it. They say, "when you meet the love of your life, time stops." When I met her, I knew it was true. Her every blink of an eye felt like months, her smile visaged like newly blossomed flowers and how her eyes shone everytime she stared at me. My heart screamed she's the most beautiful thing I have ever seen or encountered in my life.

It's kind of crazy if you think about it. Like how two complete strangers are just destined to be together. How imperfect they might be, they find perfectness in their love, how damaged and broken they might be, they heal and help each other. How there is no forced chemistry, just a pure and raw connection on its own. How they both look at each other and smile like they both have found a secret the whole world is searching for. Crazy, right? One don't just fall in love with that someone. They fall in love with their little things too. Like the sound of their laughter, the mystery of their deep eyes, the way they gaze at you and shyly look away. They make small things everything for you. They make the ordinary, extraordinary.

Our first meet wasn't really even a "date"-date . We had just met and both wanted to spend time in the city. It was one of those absolutely magical days where the conversation is effortless and you end up talking for long and bearing your soul to someone you just met. At one point, she took my hand and I knew right then that she would have the best of me. She then took me to some local cafe where we had few slices of pizza---me being a low-key fan of the junks but this kid is ought to heed his lady master today. The pizza apparently wasn't worth the taste, for all the struggles we did for it.

"I love you," She whispered, taking my hand in the warm yellow glow of the sunset. "Yes," I said, holding them tightly for I can't afford to part ways with them anyday. Sunsets are actually just a tiny bit staged, but they are staged because you want to show someone exactly how they make you feel. Sunsets are for those moments you know you'll never forget. It was the most beautiful view that I have seen in a while. I was more than happy to wake up with 4 hours of sleep, walk for miles to get a glimpse of this. While we went past some vilage during that serene evening, there came up a group of little kids playing and having fun. She then came forward and started interacting, shook hands with them and asked their names. That's when I fell completely in love with this dainty woman and felt the luckiest person on earth to have her around.

> *"All of these firsts felt so very special. So much so that you wished you could just treasure them forever and keep them locked in your mind."*

Enter Caption

CHAPTER THREE

THE ZOO

10/10/2021

you feel lonely when you're away from your parents especially when it is your first time leaving them, but there's this feeling that everything you've done so for is so much worth it, and you deserve the best world can offer. Yes im talking about her. Someone who brings out the best in me any day, someone who's closest to a 'soulmate' that I've ever met.

Meeting her is a calm certainity. Afterall for all the prayers God successfully endorsed, it feels home and comfortably safe. Do you know that 'ringing bell' thing, which they say, the moment you feel that you are in love, your inner voice sings and you hear to the music all around and the sound of ringing bells, saying that"yes. This is it"? Ever? Welp it hapened with me.

It's 10 AM in the mornng, woke up late apparently after a tiring but beautiful day. Maybe I'm sober enough to overthink while I prepare myself to meet her today. I started wondering if we all cry a little everyday. I think I do but no one actually gets to see that. Certainly, yes. My heart starts racing, my chest feels heavy and I sometimes even feel emotions climbing up to my eyes, I clench my fist sometimes and then everything settles down. Sometimes it doesn't and I continue to feel that way. I think if I were better at expressing myself, I would have cried very often. And crying helps, it used to. Until people told me that it's not good for grown ups to cry. I don't want to grow anymore on days, hope this process were ephimeral and the worldly obligations had not piled on me. The desire for a good career, the desire to be in company of good people, the desire to be the one among best. Staying away from home, in a world where men tell men, and women tell men "Crying makes you look weak" taught me not to let myself cry. How ironic when I'm typing this with my eyes little wet and scared of the fact that no one gets to see me, this way not even her.

The door knocked for i've ordered breakfast, I started eating it. And again I got too engrossed in looking at boiled milk, which looked more like my emotions, boiling but not quiet enough to spill over. I wish to spill my milk someday and no one should see it. I wish to spill it someday, people can see it and I won't get embarrassed or weak when they do.

Munching on my toasts, sipping on milk and delighted with the fact that She's the most excting and beautiful thing happened to me for she's the one who made me realise how true love is totally different from what I've seen in movies and read in books. Unreal and heavenly.

While I put on this new fit, my last t-shirt smells of her for she placed her head on my shoulder last evening. It's 1400 already and she is suppposed to be here, girls aren't punctual, changed my mind but fine. We are ought to explore the city, and it's some local zoo she agreed to visit. Never been a big fan of zoos but I can wager it's all going to be fun.

As we reached the Zoo, she held my hands, our conversation lulled, we just talked about the animals and how dainty some birds were. Moreover, how the sight of crocodiles scared her and how she smiled and teased me by coming across a monkey playing around. All this happened while I can feel the warmth of her hands in mine, for she seemed to be pretty much thrilled. The stay at Zoo barely lasted an hour as the day was about to end and we didn't want to risk reaching our places late.

"Anything that makes you go "woah, look at that" a lot will make for a good day."

CHAPTER FOUR

HER

11/10/2021

Are relationships really tiring? I guess not. A true Relationship is like a crystal clear glass. There is complete transparency. But, when a crack appears, the glass is never the same. Instead of ending things at the first sign of crack why not go through it together and come out strong, if at all the bond is strong and your partner is worth the effort? Why fear a painful ending and finish it soon instead of going an extra mile and see what beautiful times lies ahead?

> *"Why can't people just look at the crack as a design on their otherwise plain glass?*
> *After all, not all cracks are big enough to break your glass."*

It's 7 AM in the morning, She must be asleep while i'm writing this. Wish i could just straight away phone call and tell her the plethora of love my heart has submittted to. It's not just a regular day-day to me. I'm going to see her again in few hours and every cell of my body feels absolutely enlivened. This glass of water I'm drinking is the most satisfying thing I've ever consumed in my life but I am guzzling it like a hiker that has been lost alone in the desert for a week. Okay, maybe not quite that greedily, but I'm burning through it either way.

> *"You know that place between sleep and awake, that place where you still remember dreaming? That's where I'll always love you."*

It's 11 AM in the morning, she's right outside my place, I get up to go outside and walk by her, we lock eyes for a second and get stuck there. There is this feeling of butterflies with razor blade wings fluttering around in my belly. Life feels distilled to its very pure essence. She passed on a smile to me and blinked her eyes more frequently than ever, something she usually does.

I could sit here and describe her half smile, the little mole on her left cheek, I could tell you about the one stray hair bang that hung out of place. I could tell you about any of those things in great detail. She had that kind of contagious smile. The contagious laugh. I have no artistic, poetic words to describe how I felt—because there aren't any. I couldn't compare her to Helen or even to Eve or Aphrodite: she was herself, and no other. I like how her black hair curves around her cheek. How her eyebrows jump whenever she sees me. Her eyes, black as night and just as beautiful-- are always exploring. Her smile. Her smile most of all. And that was all alluringly enough.

It's after then that we planned to visit a nearby Gurudwara which somehow ended as a plan, due to some obvious reasons. However, we ended up in a cafe of her choice again! and I'd say this time she chose something cute, I did grin a bit.

The day again ended pretty well. What else one can expect when you've a once in a lifetime gem around you? nothing but utter bliss and sheer luck.

Enter Caption

CHAPTER FIVE

FOUND THE HOME IN YOU

12/10/2021

Love can make you do crazy things, enable you to make sacrifices even. And that's the beautiful part. Here I'm sacrificing my sleep writing the journal for today. Of course can't afford missing on writing one good moment with her. Indeed. The very fact that our meeting happened has already gushed in few ounces of extra blood in me. I look so pumped up with an ineveitable glow.

It's 9:00 in the morning, while I enjoy the omelette with a loaf of toasted bread, my phone beeps. She has texted me some message regarding her busy schedule and how we would not be able to meet today. I know she can't always be there for me, and things get better once you start respecting decisons. That's how relations inculcate and that's how they're supposed to. Understanding and healthy. In a nutshell mutually supportive.

Love is about a lot of things —

Fighting with each other

Being slightly possessive

Teasing your partner

More importantly,

Being considerate about their feelings and insecurities

Being expressive about how you feel for them

Making them feel special

And most importantly

After a tough day, which is inevitable when you love someone, it's about getting back to each other and making things okay. There will always be difficult times, but together you need to endure it and go past the phase.

Why? Because they're worth it.

Every second of them is worth it.

For me, loving someone is feeling a sense of "home" in their arms, or when I look into their eyes. It's caring about their time and happiness as much as I care about my own and so wanting to be the best version of myself for them.

CHAPTER SIX

THE FINAL DAY

13/10/2021

It's 13th of October already and by any chance did I realise this week run past. It felt like I was here with her since months and weeks. Like we never lived far. I know it's going to be hard for me to bid her a goodbye, for there evidently is no way to say a 'goodbye'.

She is small, 5′2″ with small chubby hands. I can still feel them on my shoulders, on my hands, my face.She wasn't crying. She is really strong or maybe she was just trying her best because I was inside the vehicle and the other one has to save the day for both of us.

I know I'll be just at a distance of three hours from her, and I'll meet her again a month.

"*The very feeling of being able to count days is comforting.*"

But when you have no time frame to look forward to, it hurts.

I remained in the cab facing her with my face buried in my left elbow trying my best to keep my tears, while she stood out near the window staring at me, for seconds. And as she started to walk away I wiped my tears off and looked at her through narrow slits of my eyes. She looked so warm. I found my solace in her. I was too anxious to let her go because something told me that "Things Change" and my heart was not ready to believe in the otherwise.

I knew we would call everyday, I will be able to see her media everyday. We will be in the same country and I can visit her once in every two months or something. I did too. I actually did visit her straight after seventeen days and that I wager, the time period felt like hours. As if I have never went for once and was all there with her.

These small things matter. Even more when they don't happen anymore. I'll miss standing at her place waiting for her while gets ready. I won't know how fast her eyes are blinking at the moment and how cute her smile looks for I always pointed out her habit of frequent and smooth blinking of eyes, however pretty. The most beautiful experiences in our lives leave the biggest dent when they get over.

I looked up and she wasn't there. My car moved. It pained so much and I knew I couldn't hug her, couldn't get to see any of her.

And this was the end of my journey. The day as well as the amazing five days that I had spent with this most beautiful person to ever exist. The five days of my life that are forever stuck in the compass of my brain, too strongly attached to ever leave. And I cherish it.

> *"You ask me the best person I've ever known and I will talk to you about her for a good one day. She will always be an integral part of my heart and I am happy to keep it safe because this is something which I can keep constant."*

It's going to be same, you know we just won't see each other everyday.

Enter Caption

CHAPTER SEVEN

STARS IN HER EYES

It was all perfect and divine
    for all the moments there were only you and mine.
    The smell of your hair,
    The light of your smile,
    Of all the places I looked for you;
    found you walking by my side.
    In the autumn sky with the settting sun,
    saw you link with kids on october one-one.
    The happy children and your company,
    sounded like a melodious symphony,
    Of all the places I looked for you;
    found you walking by my side.
    The charm of birds,
    and the fright of leopard;
    The warmth of your hands,
    the smile of love
    the sun in your eyes.
    Felt like the season that last for an age when it stayed.
    I remember you most in the starlight above,
    for all the prayers I offer,
    one part will belong to you,
    It's my vow.
    Of all the places I looked for the girl
    with the stars in her eyes.
    In the end;
    I found her walking by my side.

CHAPTER EIGHT

THE LAST MESSAGE

The day you'll read this, I might be either very much closer to your heart or nowhere near it for things change. You won't know I bought a new pair of shoes, you won't point out how no hair on my head looks so unusual, you won't hear what sports I played last evening, I won't know that you gained more weight and has started smoking cigarettes again, I won't know you just pulled cough again. These small things matter. Even more when they don't happen anymore.

You are still the first person who comes to my mind when someone asks "whom do you trust the most?". It's of course you.

"Everything looks simpler and clearer in hindsight. But there is no point in always brooding about the possible future while letting your present slip away."

And if you ask me, is it really easy to type all this from the comfort of my chair sitting alone in one room, immersed and reminiscing about our days together? No. My heart aches while typing this.

Because, One day, you decide to build a house with someone. Together, you and her put the first brick, look at each other and smile. Every single day, you and her keep adding the bricks one after the other. Sometimes, because of bad weather, some of your bricks fall down. But together, you never let the house crumble. You put those bricks back at their correct places and continue building the house.

Slowly, it starts transforming into something beautiful and unique, something you saw in a dream and now watch it happening right in front of you. It takes your breath away. All this, because you still love and cherish the idea of being in it together. And suddenly things start taking a toll, because, there comes a time, when building that house gets tiring and doesn't seem to be worth it anymore. Because the dreams once you saw together doesn't seem to be happening anymore. And then you start spending time rebuilding than living! that's when things start changing.

And this realisation that we are changing.

How can it not be painful.

When We Met

Did you know
That in your eyes there are ten thousand stars?
I would know, for into them I have fallen,
For it seems I have fallen
For the girl with the stars in her eyes.
I remember your smile with the sun in your eyes,
the smell of the autumn and your laughter tastes like sunshine.
Blooming at the sight of your radiant grace.

I remember the feel of the grass at our back,
    And the touch of its warmth, and the cool of the shade,
    And the calls of the cuckoo from the broad-way track,
    And the season that last for an age when it stayed.

Changes

Love is not an easy thing, this has been established since God knows when, but is it really that difficult? Or do we make it as though it's hard? Basic human emotions are often masked into this quality which is considered as something ill. Being emotionally raw and vulnerable is fine, being too sensitive is fine and I resent the idea of people bringing people down for feeling.

We're human beings and we're going on because we have the power of showing what we're feeling; sadness, happiness, excitement, anger, fear. All these emotions and all the vulnerability serves as a reminder that you are human, you are unique and you are special.

You will fall apart but you will get back together and rise and grow and change and become better versions of yourselves. Your life is not defined by the onlookers but you, you who lived through all the highs and lows, all the sad moments and all the happy moments. Don't let anyone tell you who you are because you know who you are and you know what you deserve.

Be raw, be comfortable, let down the shield and let people into your life. Let them love you like you love them, give them your good days and give them your bad ones.

To grow and to cherish change is the best thing you can do to yourself. To grow as a person and to become new versions of yourselves is a good thing, do not let anyone tell you otherwise. Sometimes, we have to let go of things most precious to us just to grow and evolve, like that blankie you had a hard time giving up when you were 5. Look at you now, without that blankie, you're doing perfectly fine. All you need is time, give it time and everything will heal.

If you ever decide to love someone do it whole heartedly and give them all you have, be there for them in their bad days and celebrate with them in their good ones. Give them everything you had to give, give them the world, be kind, love like you've never loved before.

Sometimes people will hate the very qualities they loved about you and this will lead you to feel guilty but if you gave them your all and you lifted them up, you were never wrong. You can never love too much; just the wrong people.

Vulnerability is a warm fire in this world which is getting colder by the day. To spread warmth through kindness, vulnerability and love in this world is not wrong. So be who you are, be loving, be sensitive, be kind, be unapologetically you. The people who love you will never stop you from being a warm ray of hope. Let your path be guided by the light in your soul and the warmth in your heart.

Live for the good days when the sky is bright blue, for the spontaneous adventures , for the ones that got away, for skills , for family and for yourself . So don't tell me that there isn't any reason to live. On a bad day think about the little positive things: Are you alive? Are you breathing? Can you smile? Can you see? Can you smell? Can you feel?Can you speak?

Think about all the things you're ABLE to do and then think about how bad your day was, it ALWAYS gets better and you WILL get better. Each day you're more experienced and wiser than yesterday and that's the only thing that's never going to change. Time is a subjective sense of becoming.You're something a nano-second before and you'll be something a nano-second later .You learn everyday, you grow everyday and I think that's amazing. I think the idea of us having the capability to show what we feel and the capability to perceive and learn is majestic and we should be grateful.

There will be days where you won't be able to get out of bed, days where you don't know who you are, days where the sun feels sharper and the moonlight feels dimmer but it's just a day and it will pass. Go outside, watch the trees, the birds, the wind rustling the leaves. The beauty of nature is that it doesn't need anything in return and it's incredible.

I see people all around me and wonder if they're happy, are they satisfied, are they comfortable? You schedule your happiness, people do what they do to gain something out of it. I can't remember life feeling authentic anymore because the world we live in now lacks time, lacks adventure, lacks love. I resent the idea of sacrificing our youth as we grow older; we have to hold on to the wonder in the back of our minds, the urge to explore and marvel because we deserve it. We deserve to feel happy, we deserve to be youthful. "You don't have to grow up to grow."

Enjoy your youth till the day you die because I plan on doing so. The idea of living the same day over and over scares me. That is what people before us have been doing and it scares me to think that we might end up like that. They say our generation is lazy and that we like things handed to us but I don't think we're lazy, I think we see the world differently and I think we're more innovative and can actually prevent living the same day over and over again.